My Napoleon

CATHERINE BRIGHTON

The Millbrook Press Brookfield, Connecticut

This is the true story of two very different people: the Emperor Napoleon Bonaparte (who was in his time the most feared and powerful general in the world), and little Betsy Balcombe (who was unknown to anyone except, of course, her family and friends). In 1815, Napoleon, who had conquered most of Europe, lost the Battle of Waterloo and surrendered to the British.

They chose to keep the world's most important prisoner on the island of St. Helena. Betsy lived on St. Helena and it was to her father's house that Napoleon came to live. He was free to move about the island because there was no means of escape, for St. Helena lay far out in the Atlantic Ocean.

Betsy's story, told here as excerpts from her journal, is based on Recollections of the Emperor Napoleon, which Betsy wrote under her married name, Mrs. Abell, later in life.

Tonight after dinner (turtle stew again, ugh!) Papa told us about our Very Important Prisoner, Napoleon. The V.I.P.N. is arriving tomorrow! I imagine him to be a huge giant with one large, flaming eye and chains around his ankles.

Papa says he is a demon, so perhaps he has a very long, pointed tail with poison on the end. I must keep my distance!

Why must he stay in *our* house? I shall never sleep, that is for sure.

The V.I.P.N. is tiny – no bigger than me!
But oh dear, he looks so very angry.

I was shy when we were introduced,
but suddenly he brushed his hair high
and made the most horrid face at me.
Then he ran in circles around the room
howling most dreadfully!

Goodness, I must have looked
perplexed, because he said, "Eh, Meez
Betzee, is this not the way an ogre
behaves?" Then he kissed me on both
cheeks and pinched my nose.

I think we shall be friends.

Napoleon will not talk to anyone but me! We speak in French, which pleases him. This evening he introduced me to his servant, who made balloons just to amuse me.

Then Napoleon showed me a tiny carriage he had made. It had four real mice to pull it! But the mice were so terrified they would not move, so he tweaked their tails. We watched the mice scamper away and Napoleon pinched my nose with delight.

Today, Napoleon took me to see his machine for making water into ice. There is no ice on our island, so I did not realize how cold it was going to be.

What an ogre he is! He put a lump of freezing ice into my mouth and then laughed to see my face as I spat it all down my dress. But I took my revenge by cutting an embroidered bugle from his coat and running away with it.

I can run faster than Napoleon — who, it must be said, is rather fat!

The most exciting day of my whole life – Napoleon took me for a canter in his carriage!

Mama would have been horrified to see how fast we went. The wheels hardly touched the ground. Napoleon often glanced at me. He hoped I would be frightened, but the faster he went, the more I laughed.

"*Mon Dieu*, Mademoiselle Betsy, you are the wildest little girl!" he said, when we arrived home. "I have seen generals who cannot compare with you."

Goodness, I felt proud.

Napoleon loves to tease me. Today
he made me kiss a horrid boy who
came to visit, and was delighted when
my face went red.

He is not my friend anymore.
I refuse to speak to him ever, ever, ever.
I have been plotting my revenge.

I took my revenge, but it ended
in disaster.

We were all out walking in
single file. Napoleon was at the front,
which is where a general likes to
be, and I was at the back. I pushed
the horrid boy, who fell forward,
knocking over his stuck-up father,
who in turn fell over and knocked
over Napoleon – who fell into a
prickly pear bush!

I laughed and laughed to see
Napoleon covered in thorns, but
when Papa heard of my joke, he
said he would punish me.

Oh, what a punishment: Papa locked me in the cellar all night. It was dark and damp. Most horrid of all, there were rats!

I cowered in the corner until I spied Papa's rack of best claret. All night long I threw claret bottles at the rats, until morning came and I was released.

Papa was not pleased when he saw his precious wine everywhere, but when Napoleon heard about it, he laughed and laughed.

We are friends again.

Tonight I dined with Napoleon. We had turkey galantine, which was delicious. I must have looked funny as I ate, for he laughed at me.

"You English are only used to roast beef, Mademoiselle Betsy," he said. "Now, this is real food."

I could not resist replying that I knew the French only ate frogs! He looked most indignant. Then he insisted on feeding me delicious sugar bonbons: one for him, one for me. I felt quite ill and was sick all over his Turkish carpet.

What a disgrace!

Today I felt better and promised poor Mama that I would behave more like a lady (although, I fear, that would be boring). In the afternoon, I visited Napoleon.

"Ah, Mademoiselle Betsy, not so green today?" he asked, and pinched my nose. Then he gave me a lesson in how to shoot a real gun and win a battle. This last lesson involved setting up his giant chess pieces on the lawn in battle formation. I loved it!

Napoleon cheated, so of course I lost.

Disaster has struck: Mama is ill and we must return to England.

When I went to see Napoleon, he had already heard the news. We sat in silence and played bézique. He opened a box of my favorite bonbons, but they stuck in my throat next to the big lump of my tears.

Napoleon has said "I love you" to many beautiful women, I am sure, but I must be the only little girl to hear those words from him.

This is what Napoleon said to me as we stood on the quay:

"Mademoiselle Betsy, are you really sailing away to England and leaving me here on this miserable rock? Look at those cruel mountains — they are my prison walls.

"I shall die here. You will soon hear that the Emperor Napoleon is dead."

He gave me a lock of his hair and a little snuff box, which I will treasure for ever and ever and ever.

Goodbye, Emperor!

Napoleon died on St. Helena shortly after Betsy left.

NAPOLEON'S *biography*

1769 *Born in Ajaccio, Corsica*

1784-5 *Trained to be an artillery officer at the École Militaire in Paris*

1793-5 *Commanded artillery during the siege of Toulon and helped
put down an uprising in Paris
Became a general commanding the army in France*

1796 *Married Josephine de Beauharnais*

1796-7 *Led the French army in northern Italy against Austria*

1798 *Captured Malta and won the battle of the Pyramids in Egypt*

1799 *Appointed one of three consuls to rule France, then First Consul*

1800 *Defeated the Austrians at Marengo in Italy*

1804 *Crowned Emperor Napoleon 1*

1805-7 *Planned, then abandoned invasion of England
Defeated the Austrian army at Ulm, the Austrian / Russian
army at Austerlitz, the Prussian army at Jena and the
Russian army at Friedland*

1808-9 *Commanded the French army in Spain and defeated the Austrian
army at Wagram*

1810 *Divorced Josephine to marry the Archduchess Marie-Louise of Austria*

1811 *Birth of a son, Napoleon*

1812 *Invaded Russia, winning battles at Smolensk and Borodino.
Entered Moscow with about 453,000 men, most of whom died
during the Russian winter*

1813 *Defeated by an allied army at Leipzig and withdrew to France*

1814 *Abdicated as emperor and exiled to the island of Elba*

1815 *Escaped from Elba
Defeated at the battle of Waterloo and abdicated a second time
Exiled to St. Helena, arriving there on 15 October*

1821 *Died at St. Helena on 5 May*

beast feast

poems and paintings by

Douglas Florian

voyager books
harcourt brace & company
SAN DIEGO   NEW YORK   LONDON

First Voyager Books edition 1998
Voyager Books is a registered trademark of Harcourt Brace & Company.

Library of Congress Cataloging-in-Publication Data
Florian, Douglas.
Beast feast/Douglas Florian.—1st ed.
p. cm.
"Voyager Books."
Summary: A collection of humorous poems about such animals
as the walrus, anteater, and boa.
ISBN 0-15-295178-4
ISBN 0-15-201737-2 pb
1. Animals—Juvenile poetry. 2. Children's poetry, American. [1. Animals—Poetry.
2. Humorous poems. 3. American poetry.] I. Title.
PS3556.L589B4   1994
811'.54—dc20   93-10720

PRINTED IN SINGAPORE

H J L N O M K I G

Contents

The Walrus

The pounding spatter
Of salty sea
Makes the walrus
Walrusty.

8

The Barracuda

In all the world
Nothing's ruder
Than a hungry
Barracuda.

9

The Anteater

The
    anteater's
        long
           and
               tacky
                   tongue
                       is
                           snaking
                               from
                                   its
                                 snout.

A thousand termites riding in,
But no one riding out.

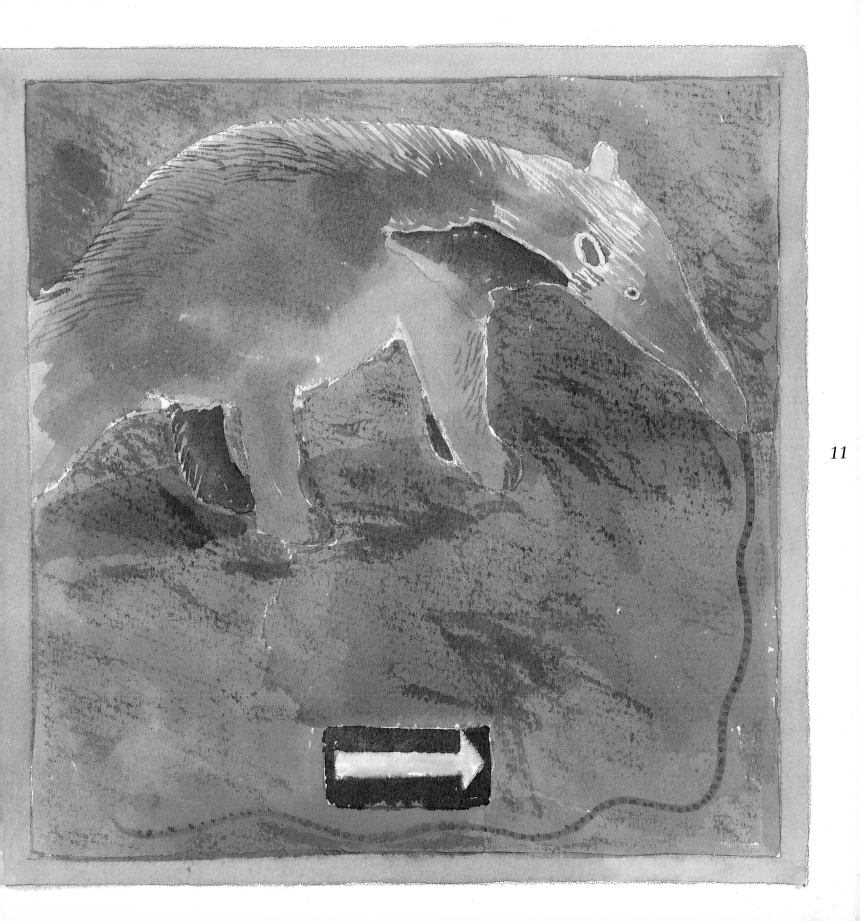

The Boa

Just when you think you know the boa,
There's moa and moa and moa and moa.

The Lobster

See the hard-shelled
Leggy lobster
Like an underwater
Mobster
With two claws
To catch and crush
Worms and mollusks
Into mush
And antennae
Long and thick
Used for striking
Like a stick.
So be careful
On vacation
Not to step on
This crustacean.

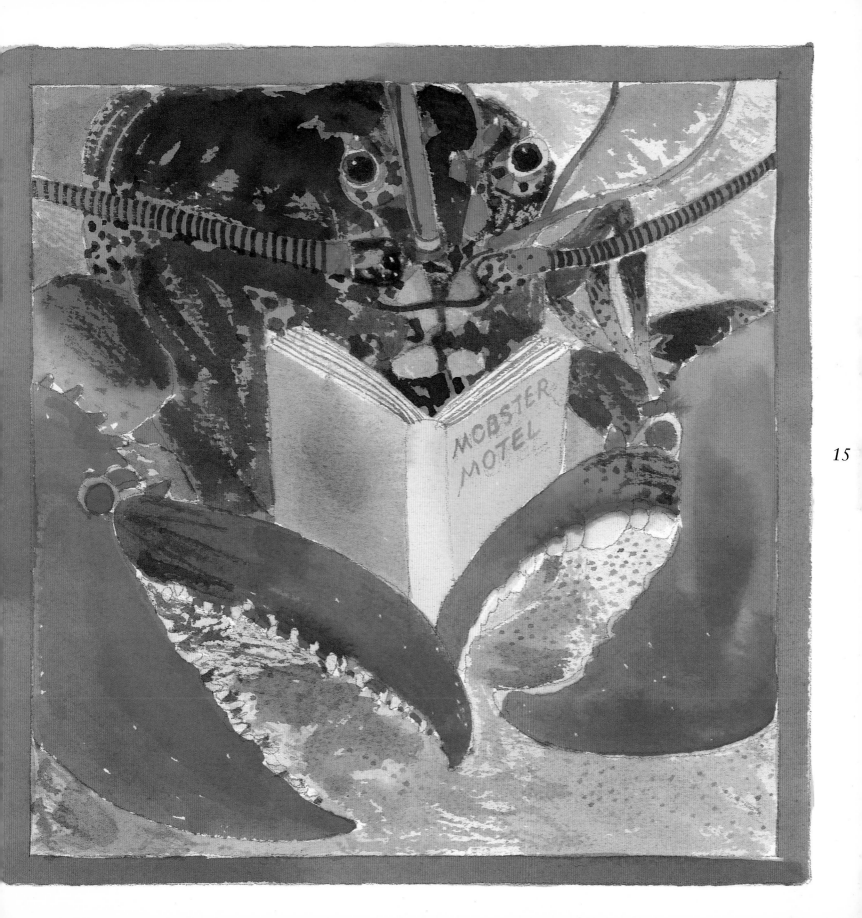

16

The Chameleon

Although it may seem very strange,
The colors on a chameleon change
From mousy browns to leafy greens
And several colors in between.
Its very long and sticky tongue
On unsuspecting bugs is sprung.
It lashes out at rapid rates
On unaware invertebrates,
Then just as quickly will retract
With flabbergasted fly intact.
So bugs beware this risky reptilian —
The clever everchanging chameleon.

The Rhea

The rhea rheally isn't strange —
It's just an ostrich, rhearranged.

The Ants

Ants are scantily
Half an inch long,
But for their size
They're very strong.
Ants tote leaves
Five times their weight
Back to their nest
At speedy rate.
They walk on tree limbs
Upside down
A hundred feet
Above the ground,
While down below
Beneath a mound
They're building tunnels
Underground.
And so it's been —
And it will be —
Since greatest
Ant antiquity.

The Whale

Big as a street —
With fins, not feet —
I'm full of blubber,
With skin like rubber.
When I breathe out,
I s p e w a spout.
I swim by the shore
And eat more and more.
I'm very, very hard to ignore.

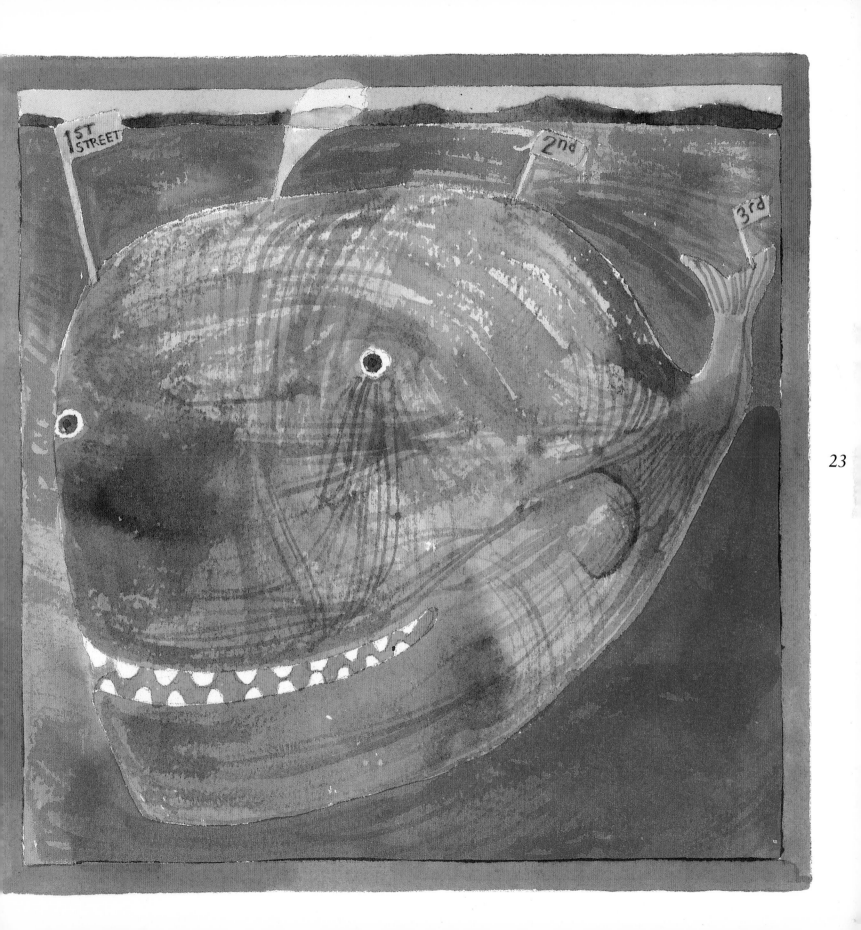

23

24

The Pigeon

I don't claim to
Love the pigeon,
But I like it
Just a smidgen.
Pigeons don't get
No respect
Just because they
Hunt and peck.
When they walk
Their heads go bobbin' —
You don't see that
In a robin.
They will sit right
On your shoulder.
Not too many
Birds are bolder.
Just be thankful
They're around
To pick up crumbs
Left on the ground.

The Armadillo

The armadillo
As a pillow
Would really be swell
Except
For the fact
That it comes in a shell.

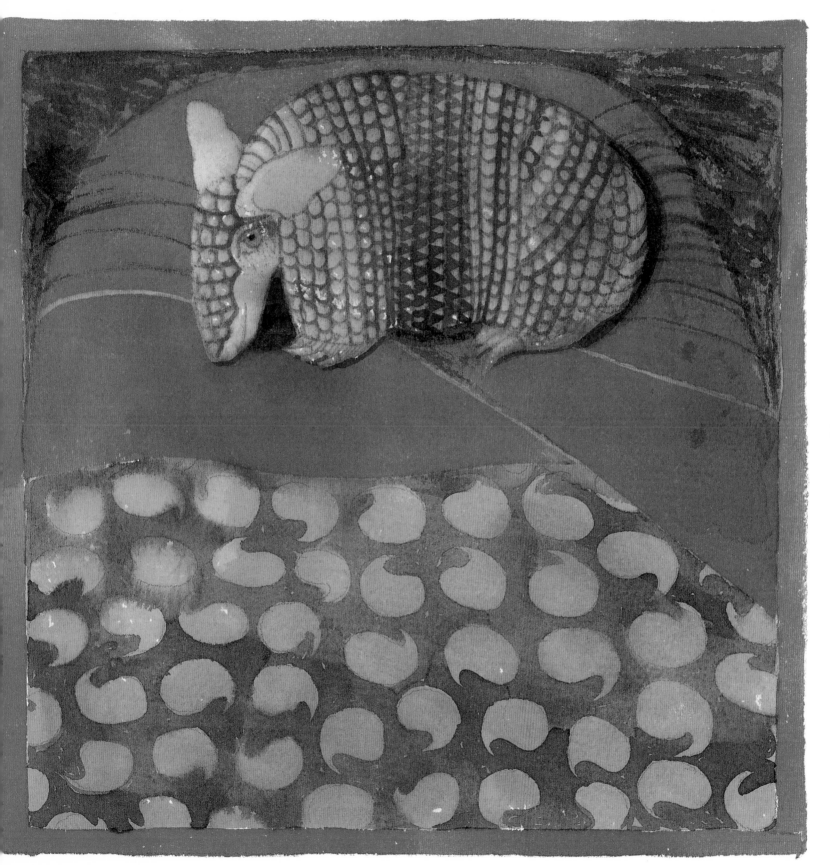

The Sloth

Up in a tree
The shaggy sloth
Is hanging by its claws.
It doesn't like to move at all.
It only likes to
p a u s e.

The Grasshopper

Green as a leaf.
Fast as a thief.
My olive eyes are
O v e r s i z e d.
My two antennae
Grow and spread
Like tapered threads
Upon my head.
I hatch from eggs
With springs in my legs
And grind on grasses
As
    summer
        passes.

The Camel

The camel's altogether scary
With features haggard, harsh, and hairy.
It has a long and crooked neck
And giant feet to help it trek
Across the hot, dry desert sands
And over Asian prairie lands.
Upon its back a hairy hump
Arises like a beastly bump.
But do not fear the dreary camel.
It's not a monster —
It's a mammal.

The Caterpillar

The caterpillar's not a cat.
It's very small
And short and fat,
And with those beady little eyes
Will never win a beauty prize.
The caterpillar's brain is small —
It only knows to eat and crawl.
But for this creepy bug don't cry,
It soon will be a butterfly.

The Toad

The tubby toad's so squat and plump
That rarely does it even jump.
At night it feeds on worms and slugs,
Small spiders and assorted bugs,
Then hops into an earthy burrow
To dream of catching more tomorrow.

The Bat

The bat is batty as can be.
It sleeps all day in cave or tree,
And when the sun sets in the sky,
It rises from its rest to fly.
All night this mobile mammal mugs
A myriad of flying bugs.
And after its night out on the town,
The batty bat sleeps

Upside down.

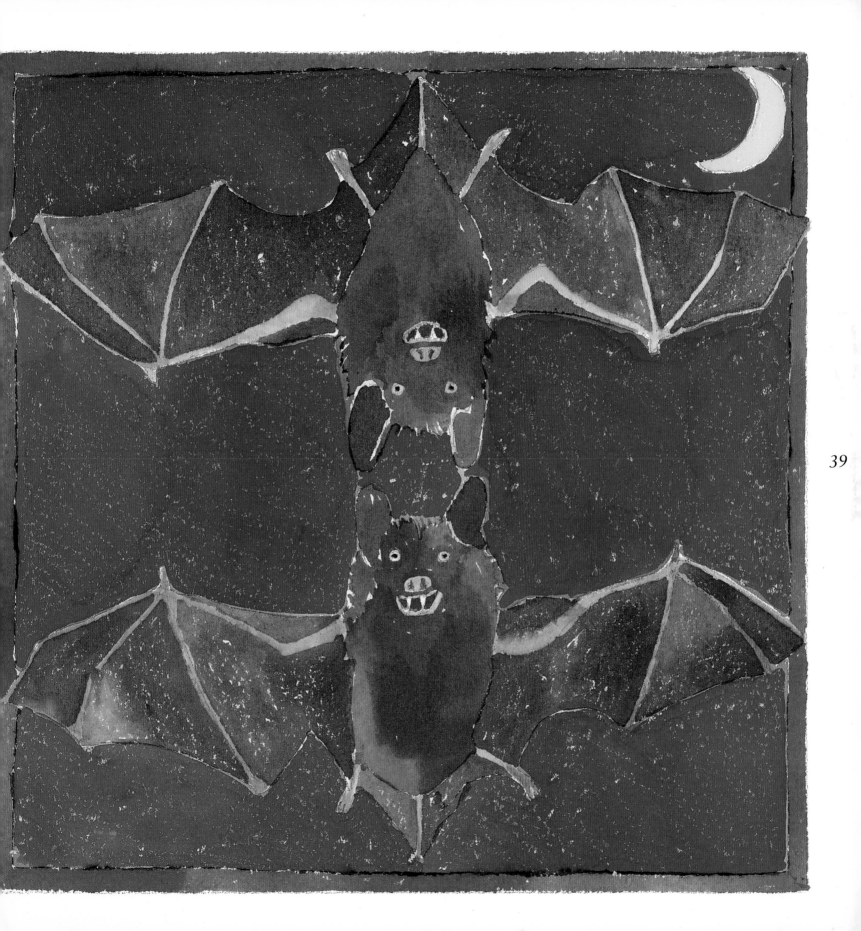

39

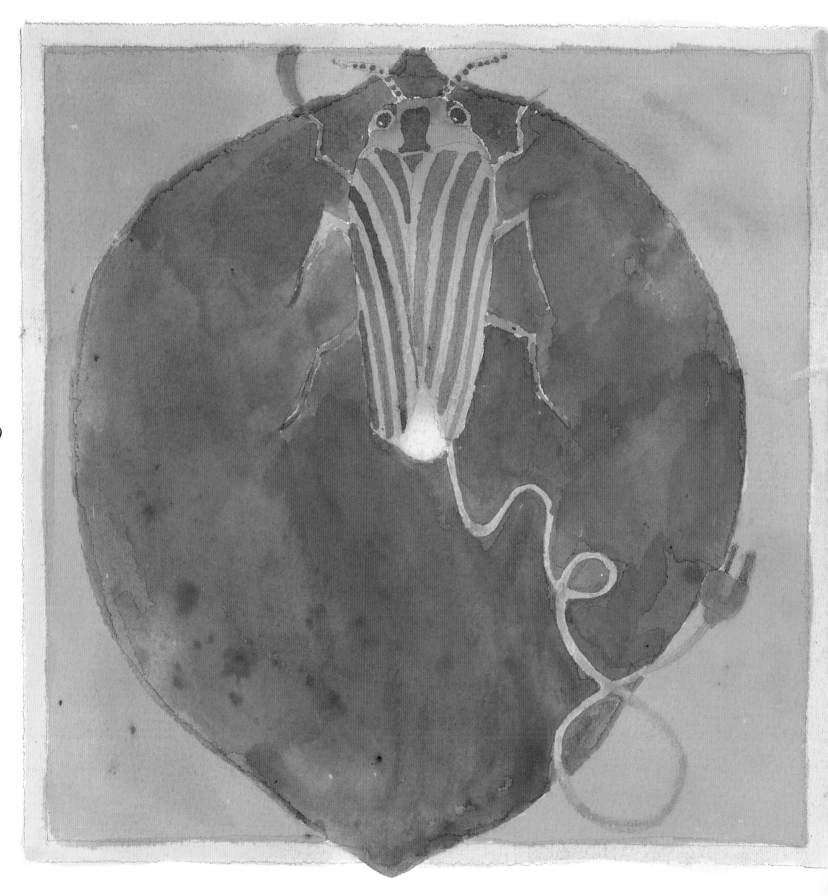

40

The Firefly

On August nights
The firefly lights
Blink
ON and OFF
Amongst the trees
But have no need
For batteries.

The Kangaroo

The kangaroo loves to leap.
Into the air it zooms,
While baby's fast asleep
Inside its kangaroom.

43

44

The Mole

The mole digs a hole with its toes
With help from its long pointed nose.
    By digging so thorough
    It makes a deep burrow
In which it can dreamily doze.

Its ears are not easily found
But perfect for picking up sound.
    Though virtually blind
    The mole doesn't mind —
There's not much to see underground.

The Kiwi

Wings so small.
No tail at all.
Very rare.
Feathers like hair.
Quiet and shy.
Cannot fly.
They call you a bird,
But I don't know why.

The paintings in this book were done in watercolor
on rough French watercolor paper.
The display type was set in Pabst and
the text type was set in Sabon
by Thompson Type, San Diego, California.
Color separations by Bright Arts, Ltd., Singapore
Printed and bound by Tien Wah Press, Singapore
Production supervision by Stanley Redfern and Jane Van Gelder
Designed by Lisa Peters